C0-AVX-783

HuaTao's Quick Sketches from Life Models

One to Two Minute, Five to Ten Minute, and Twenty to Thirty Minute Sketching Methods

HuaTao's Quick Sketches from Life Models

One to Two Minute, Five to Ten Minute, and Twenty to Thirty Minute Sketching Methods

HuaTao Zhang

HIH ART STUDIO
San Jose, California

Published by:

HIH ART STUDIO
P.O. Box 20621
San Jose, California 95160-0621

First published in 2006

ISBN 1-59975-378-2
LCCN 2005937503

Zhang, HuaTao
HuaTao's quick sketches from life models / HuaTao Zhang

A note from artist and author:
All the images of the sketches in this book were done from life.
All the original images were done in the size of 18 inches by 24 inches
on acid free sketch paper. The full size dimensions of all the original images
have been cropped and reduced for this book.

Text transcribed and edited by Arline Williams
(dictated by HuaTao Zhang)
Book Designed by HIH Art Studio

Printed in China 2006

Dedication

This book is dedicated to all the
masters of figure drawing through the ages, including
Rembrandt Harmenszoon van Rijn, Jean-Auguste-Dominique Ingres,
James Abbott McNeill Whistler, Anders Zorn, Gustav
Klimt, Egon Schiele, and Nicholas Feching.

I especially dedicate this book to you, the reader, for
your love and support of art.

Acknowledgments

I would like to express my deepest thanks and
appreciation to all the models who posed
so gracefully for these quick sketch drawings.
Without them, it would have been impossible to create this book.

I extend special thanks to Arline Williams for contributing
her English language skills, and her enthusiasm
to this project. Her editorial work is sincerely appreciated.

Thanks to Michael Hegglund, who encouraged me
to go forward with this project, and to Mary Ann Chuck
for her kindness and support through the early years.

Thanks also to Linda Covello, Visual Arts Director
of the Community School of Music and Arts in Mountain View, California,
for her willingness to reach beyond the known, and to
Diana Argabrite, Director of Arts and Schools at
Euphrat Museum of Art, De Anza College, Cupertino, California,
for paving the way for this book.

Most of all, my gratitude to my wife, Hong Gao,
Who supported me and kept my art going.

Contents

Preface

Two years ago, we started the open studio at the Community School of Music and Arts in Mountain View, California.

In setting up this studio, I envisioned a room full of people learning from the experience of working with a model, as well as learning from working with each other. They would see the infinite variety of approaches possible with this practice. Artists would work through a series of individually developed marks to describe the figure as they perceived it. Each perception would be unique, varying from artist to artist.

In these quick drawings HuaTao captures the essence of form. He is able to pare down the complicated rhythms of the human body into the perfect balance of structure and expression. His use of the brush in the drawings he calls "black and white" reflects his many years of practice in the calligraphic traditions of his native China, as well as his personal vision.

I am inspired by his repeated ability to capture light and form while keeping his drawings fresh and spontaneous. I know he has been inspirational to the other artists and students who draw with him and, through this book, HuaTao will be able to share his drawings with a wider audience.

Linda Covello

Visual Arts Director
Community School of Music and Arts
Mountain View, California

December 2005

Introduction

Quick Sketches from Life Models is divided into three sections.

The sections are: One to Two Minute Sketches, Five to Ten Minute Sketches, and Twenty to Thirty Minute Sketches. Each section discusses my method for achieving quick, individually interpretive sketches. I want to share my ideas with both aspiring and advanced artists. The technique and materials vary slightly for each of the three types of drawings.

A word about materials: To create a freer style I use brush and marker. I break the marker and dip the brush in the marker ink. This creates a softer medium for drawing. Usually I use regular ink or Chinese ink purchased from an art supply store. I use softer lines to capture the pose quickly. Occasionally, I use pencil but sometimes find it too stiff. I like to stay with the brush and broken marker to draw lines.

For the five to ten minute quick drawings, I introduce an ink pen with a fine point (.05mm) purchased from an office supply store. This gives more detail and information about the model's pose and form. I never use an eraser. It takes too much time to erase lines, and I may lose the mood I am trying to capture. Also, erasing my initial decision usually diminishes the finished drawing. Then, I add line and tone: I make a decision about the image and put down on paper my first impression of whatever I see and feel. This builds self-confidence. Erasing undermines that confidence.

For twenty to thirty minute sketches, the model usually relaxes or lies down to pose. First, I use pen and ink to draw the image. There are hundreds of ways to sketch. Sketching is a very individual art form with few rules. The artist's personal touches and interpretations are very unique. How you feel is how you draw. Your mood shines through your sketches.

I don't think much about anatomy while I am sketching. Of course, a sketch artist must have some knowledge of anatomy, but trying to achieve perfection in anatomical drawing will often lock the artist up. Every artist is different, and every model is different. An artist can only convey a general idea of structure for the human body. Just think about the model's pose in the way that is most comfortable to you, rather than concerning yourself with drawing correctly. For example, I know I am working in the best way for me when I feel I have lost touch with the outside world, and the world is suddenly reduced to me and the image, I am aware of nothing else.

Part One:
One to Two Minute Sketches

When the life model poses only 1-2 minutes, you have a very limited amount of time to think about anatomical structure. I follow the basic structure and achieve a line flow immediately. Normally, I begin drawing from the neck of the model and look for the contour of the body first. Then, I follow the contour line of the body. For quick sketching, most models stand up. I start the line work at the shoulder. Next, I look at how the body is twisting or turning. Gestural lines follow the movement, not the anatomy. They are the artist's first attempt to position the body and act as markers for locating and drawing the parts of the body. Then I use a few basic brush strokes to indicate position and begin to build the drawing. I note the position of the leg, arm, hand, and so on, before I start any real drawing. I warm up a little, and when I have a good feeling about the drawing, I draw the contour line anatomy. I use the knowledge gained from studying the various parts of the human body, such as muscle and bone.

I use an ink wash for shadows. Sometimes I use dry ink and sometimes wet ink, or a combination of both. Also, at the same time I use a few Chinese brush-painting techniques to enhance the quality of the lines. Sometimes, good sketch work can result in a fine piece of finished artwork. In 1-2 minute sketching, the need to draw quickly is urgent. It's good not to over analyze the sketch. Sometimes this spontaneous style will produce a "happy accident." The work develops easily and completely.

When I first started doing these sketches there was no life model available, so I used videotapes, ballet dancers, modern dancers, gymnasts, or ice skaters on TV to do quick drawings. These "models" are naturally graceful, and most of their poses are very elegant, but powerful. These drawings usually take less than one minute and allow freshness without a lot of detail.

Gestural Line Following the Movements

2 min.
Jan. 24, 2005

1 min
Nov. 15, 2004

1 min
June 6, 2005

April 24, 2005

1 min
March 21, 2005

Sep. 20, 2004

1-24-05 1 min

2 min
June 13, 2005

11-25-04 1 min.

NOV. 1ST, 2004 1 min.

1 min.
10-25-04

1 min.
10-25-04

Contour Line Following the Anatomy

1 min.
June 6, 2005
2 min.
June 6, 2005

1 min.
March 21, 2005

march 14. 05

Black and White

10/24/05 1min.

Oct. 3. 2005

1 min.
Oct. 10, 2005

Part Two:
Five to Ten Minute Sketches

During 5-10 minute sketches, most models still stand up or sit down. Positions are generally more interesting. With the longer drawing time, I start adding more detail work. I still like to use brush, or pencil, or ink wash. But for most of them, I like to use an ink pen (.05 mm). My method and style borrow heavily from a printmaking technique known as cross-hatching. The 5-10 minute drawings allow a little more time to add in more tone, shadow, and detail.

In 1-2 minute drawings, I show only the eyes, face, and body movement. For 5-10 minute sketches, I add in the nose and mouth and sometimes include details for the hands and feet.

With more time, you can set up the lighting and show more angles in the sketch. Normally, I like to set up the light sideways, to the left or right, parallel with the model, so I can add shadows in the body between the muscles and bones. Sometimes, I put the lighting on the floor. I always use one or two strong lights to show direction and a third, less prominent light to add more interesting, subtle tones. When drawing, you still must respond quickly to capture all elements, including anatomy, gesture, structure, lighting, shadows and tone.

Models still stand, sit, or lie down, allowing the artist to capture both action and detail in the sketch. This is one of my favorite aspects of the 5-10 minute sketches.

I still use ink wash to capture tone and shadow for many of these sketches. This medium presents the background and the body as a combination of black and white. Sometimes I draw the background as a device to show the body. Later, I may add a little water to the ink for tone in the body. This strategy, while still considered a sketching technique borrows from painting.

Detail Drawing

5 minutes
November 15, 2004

April 11, 2005
5 min

5 min.
Feb. 14, 2005

5 min.
Feb. 14, 2005

5 min.
February 7, 2005

5 minutes
November 15, 2004
5 min.
April 4, 2005

5 min.
June 6, 2005

5 min.
March 21, 2005

Line and Tone Studies

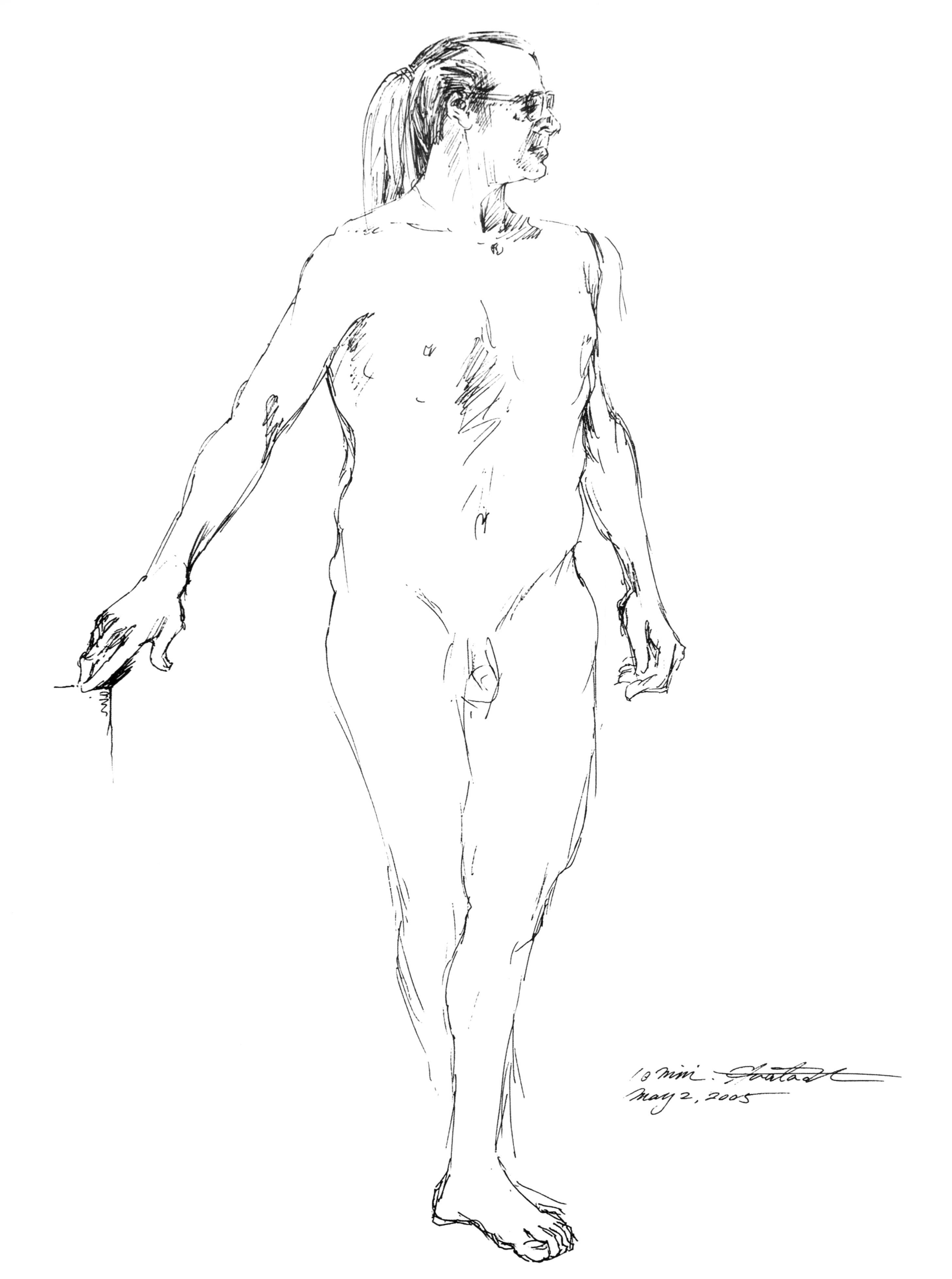
10 min.
May 2, 2005

March 7, 2005 5 min

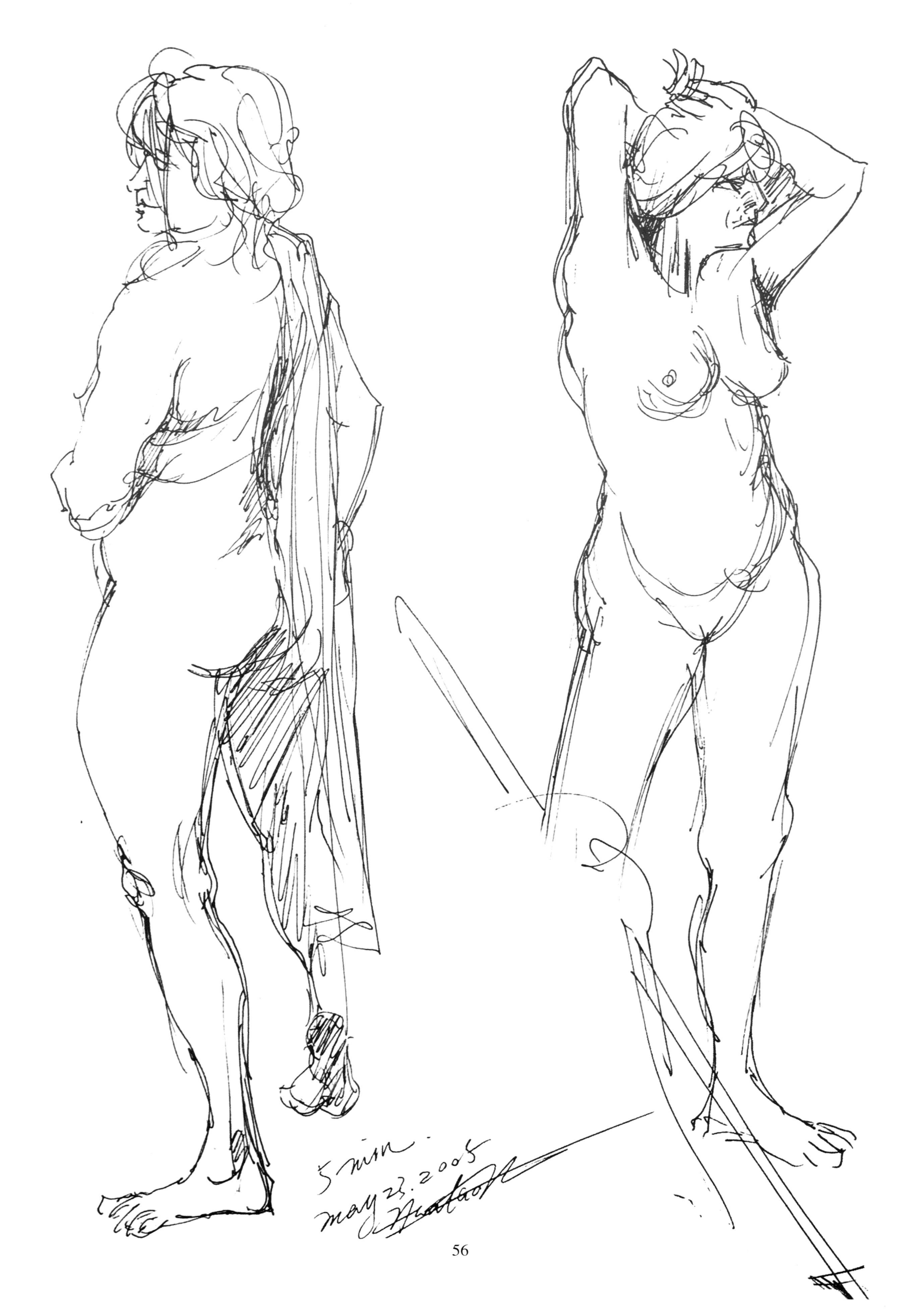
5 min.
May 23. 2005

July 18, 2005
5 min.

May 10, 2004

10-18-04

5 min.
February 7, 2005

March 14. 05
10 min.

10 minutes
November 15, 2004

10 min.
10-25-04

10-18-04

10 min. August 8. 2005

10 min. March 21, 2005

10 min.
10-25-04

Sep. 26, 2005

November 1st, 2004 10 min.

May 15, 2005
10 min.

May 9, 2005 10 min.

10 min.
June 6, 2005

November 1st, 2004 10 min.

10 min.
March 7, 2005

march 7, 2005
5 min.
Jan.18, 2005 10 min.

Ink Wash for Tone and Shadow

Oct. 3, 2005

Part Three:
Twenty to Thirty Minute Sketches

For 20-30 minute sketches, I give up the brush and use fine point ink pen, which is easier to maintain than the ink used in brush and water sketching. Remember, you cannot use an eraser. Use your confidence to make your shape and form. You are forced to make the right drawing decision each time. If you make a mistake, fine. Next time, you will make a better decision! I like using a pen, because it forces me to stretch my abilities as an artist.

For 20-30 minute sketches, the models start to relax because they are holding the pose longer. For these poses, most models will lie down, sit, or stand up. Contour lines are not really important. Study the shadows and tone. Add more detail.

The model is no longer the only source of information—you should also draw on the environment surrounding the model. Background information becomes more important in enhancing the image of the model. Because you have more time, you can include background elements around the model, such as a scarf or a chair. These details enrich the artist's sketch.

For the standing pose, I pay close attention to structure. For the lying pose, I also pay attention to perspective. Model poses are not the positions one normally finds in daily life. The models have perfected unusually artistic poses for the purpose of assisting the artist in the creation of a sketch. Many models sit on the ground, on a chair, or on a high stool. Each model has a unique way of sitting. Every model poses differently.

Lighting is especially important in the 20-30 minute sketches. Structure and anatomy becomes even more significant. One of the dangers of the longer posing time is the potential loss of freshness. My way of dealing with this is to first use the 1-2 minute method to get a very nice pose. Then, I add more detail, especially on the hands, feet and head. I even draw some of the models' expressions in the face, because the face is more important for the 20-30 minute sketches. Having more time to study the figure allows you to capture more detail. At the same time, of course, you need to study shadow and lighting, which help to define the contour shadows in the body. The final sketch may result in a finished piece of art.

Standing and Reclining Pose

July 18, 2005 20min.

20 min.
June 13. 2005

Jan. 18. 2005
20 min.

at CSMA 20min.
June 13. 2005

November 1st. 2004 20min.

Feb. 28, 2005

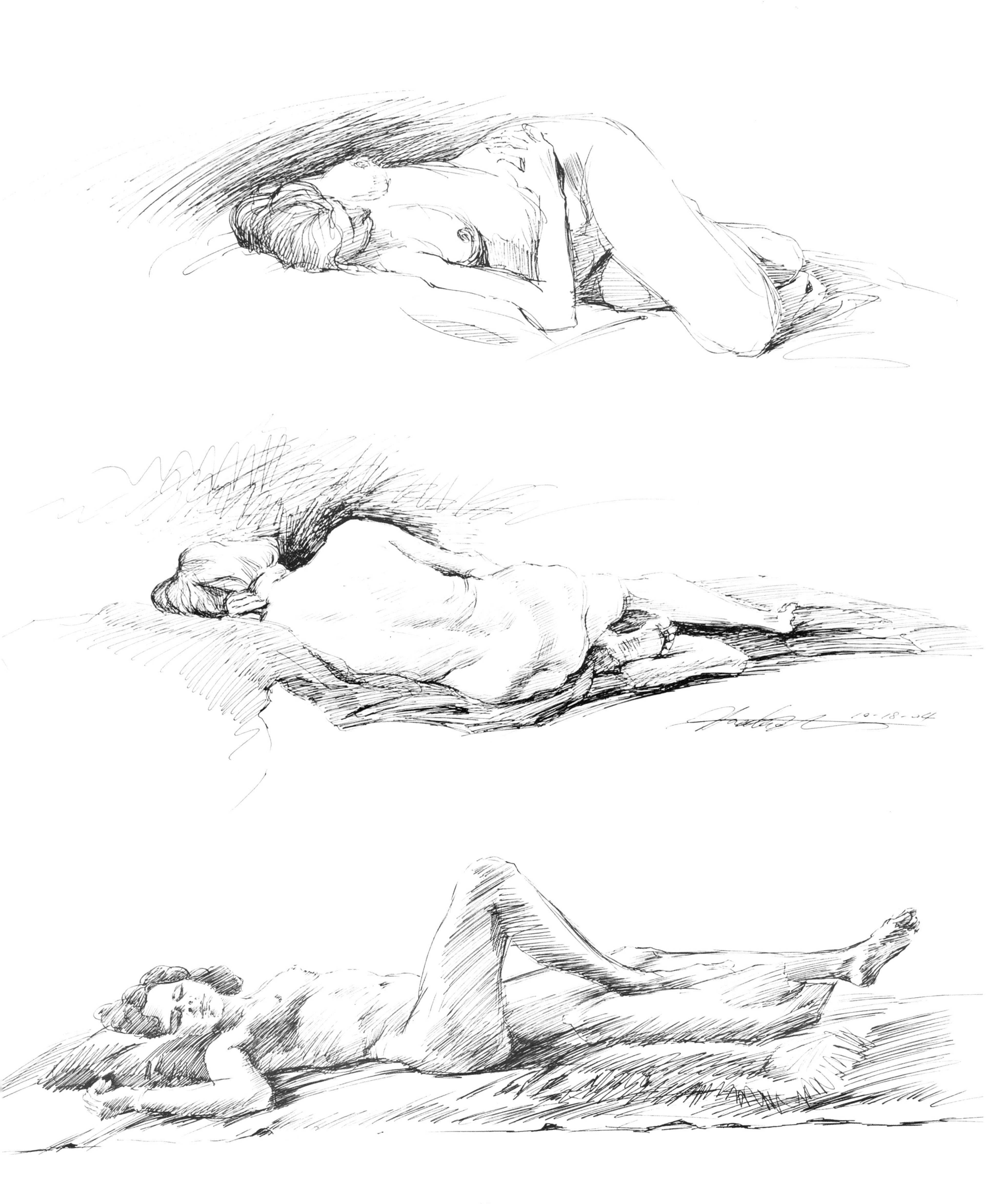

Sitting Pose

March 14, 2005 20min.

Oct. 4, 2004

Oct. 4, 2004

20 min.
June 6, 2005

12-13-04 20min

11-25-04 20 min

11-25-04 20min.

July 18, 2005
20 min.

May 10, 2004

20 minutes
November 15, 2004
20 min
August 8, 2005

20 min.
February 7, 2005

12-13-04 20 min.

July 18, 2005
20 min

April 4, 2005
20 min.

May 9, 2005 20 min.

30 min.
Jan. 24, 2005

may 9, 2005 20min.

March 14, 2005
20min.

20min
June 13. 2005

March 7, 2005 20min.

20 min.
May 23, 2005

Nov. 7, 2005 20min.

Index
Paper Sizes, Mediums and Dates